The Pizza Book

Raw Plant Based & Gluten-Free Recipes

by
Kachina Choate
Summer Bear

The Pizza Book
Raw Plant Based & Gluten-Free Recipes

Copyright © 2020 Kachina Choate

All Rights reserved. No part of this publication may be reproduced, stored in a retrieval system, or transmitted, in any form by any means, electronic, mechanical, photocopying, recording, or otherwise, without the prior written consent of the copyright owner.

dollkachina@gmail.com

First Edition 2020

ISBN (print) 978-1-938142-10-9
ISBN (eBook) 978-1-938142-11-6

1. Raw Foods 2. Cookery (Natural foods) 3. Pizza 4. Gluten-Free

Book Design: Kachina Design

This book is not intended to cure or give medical advice. Its intention is to educate, inform, and empower readers to make their own decisions on health and well-being. Each person will have unique reactions to changes in diet. If you have concerns about your health or diet, consult your healthcare advisor.

Table of Contents

- 4   *Inrtoduction*
- 5   *Pizza Recipes*
- 52   *Dessert Pizza Recipes*
- 66   *Pizza Crust Recipes*
- 73   *Miscellaneous Recipes*
- 79   *Non-Dairy Recipes*
- 90   *Index*

Introduction

My friend Cheryl was sad when she found out that she had celiac disease because it would require her to stop eating many of her favorite foods.

One day I brought her one of my pizzas. She tasted it and then burst into tears. My first thought was 'oh no...it's that bad.' I said, "what's wrong?" Though her tears she said, "I thought I would never have pizza again."

As Cheryl's tears proved pizza is a comfort food, and most people have good memories of eating pizza.

The word pizza is first found in Gaeta in 997 AD and moved through Central and Southern Italy. In the 18th century Naples added tomatoes to flat bread. According to legend pizza maker Raffaele Esposito garnished a pizza with tomatoes, mozzarella and basil to represent the colors on the Italian flag to honor the Queen Consort of Italy.

Pizza became known all over the world after the World War II allied soldiers stationed in Italy bought the recipe home.

Pizza has taken all forms and can be made from almost anything having a sweet, savory, or spicy flavor profile. They even can be made from leftovers. I had a refrigerator full of leftovers and a potluck the next day. I didn't want to buy anything for it. Being inspired by a TV commercial I created pizza bites out the leftovers.

Olive Pizza

Preparation: 30 Min. Drying: 1-3 Hrs. Makes 4-6 Servings

Ingredients

- pizza crust (page 70)

Topping:

- ½ c. sun dried olives
- ½ c. artichokes hearts (optional not a raw product)
- 1 c. nut mayo (page 80)
- ½ c red bell peppers

Sauce:

- 1 c. dried tomatoes
- 1 tbsp. pizza seasoning
- 2 tbsp. olive oil
- 1 tbsp. lemon juice

Directions

Make pizza crust and nut mayo then set aside.

Sauce:

Place tomatoes, pizza seasoning, and olive oil in a blender and mix until well combined.

Toppings:

Chop artichoke hearts. Place sauce on the dough. Layer the artichoke hearts and olives. Top by dropping mayo over the top, this becomes cheese.

Dry at 100°F. in a dehydrator for an hour or two.

Pizza Bites

Preparation: 35 Min.   Soaking: 8-12 Hrs..   Drying: 5-10 Hrs.   Makes 8-12 Servings

Ingredients

Crust

- 1 large onion, chopped
- 2-3 stalks of celery, chopped
- 3 small tomatoes, chopped
- 2-3 cloves of garlic
- 1 tsp. Himalayan crystal salt
- 2 c. golden flax, ground in coffee grinder
- water if needed

Filling

- 1 c. sunflower seeds, soaked overnight
- 1 medium onion
- 1 tbs. cold pressed olive oil

- 2 tbs. poultry seasoning
- Himalayan crystal salt

Sauce

- 4 medium tomatoes
- ½ c. dried tomatoes, soaked 20 minutes in water
- 1 tbs. pizza seasonings

Toppings

- red bell peppers
- olives
- mushrooms
- whatever else you may enjoy on pizza.

Directions

Place vegetables and salt in food processor and mix well. Slowly add ground flax. It should be doughy and dry enough to spread. Spread on nonstick dehydrator sheet about 4 inches wide and about ½ inch thick and set aside. You may need more than one nonstick dehydrator sheet.

Mix sunflower seeds, onion, olive oil, poultry seasoning, and salt in a food processor, until well mixed and spread over the crust.

Mix 4 fresh tomatoes, soaked tomatoes and pizza seasoning in blender until smooth. Spread sauce over the filling.

Spread chopped toppings over the sauce and then fold one side of the crust to the middle and then the other side to the middle.

Cut into bite sized piece and dehydrate for about 5-10 hours at a 100° F. It is done when it looks "cooked."

Fun Fact:

Charlemagne considered flax so important for the health of his subjects that he passed laws and regulations requiring its consumption in the eighth century A.D.

Kale Pizza

Preparation: *Drying:*   *Makes 4-6*
20 Min.   *60-90 Min.*   *Servings*

Ingredients

- 1 c. ricotta cheese sauce (page 85)
- ¼ c. rawmesan (page 83) or nutritional yeast
- 3 ½ c. kale
- 1 clove garlic
- 1 ½ tbsp. cold pressed olive oil
- 1 lemon, juiced
- ½ tsp. black pepper
- ¼ tsp. Himalayan crystal salt
- 1 tbsp. fresh basil
- ½ tbsp. fresh parsley
- ¼ c. onion, chopped
- ½ tsp. red pepper flakes (optional)
- ½ c. cherry tomatoes
- ¼ c. raw olives
- 2 tbsp. pure water
- pizza crust (page 70)

Directions

Make pizza crust.

In a blender, mix garlic, black pepper, basil, parsley, onion, lemon juice, and ½ tbsp. cold pressed olive oil and mix.

Remove stems from kale. Thinly slice or chop kale and place in a bowl. Pour blender mixture over kale and massage mixture in the kale with hands for 2-3 minutes, then let sit until ready to use.

Make ricotta cheese sauce. Brush 1 tbsp. olive oil over the crust. Spread about ½ cup ricotta cheese sauce on the crust.

Cover ricotta cheese sauce with marinated kale. Sprinkle tomatoes and olives over kale. Randomly place scoops of remaining ricotta cheese sauce over the top of the pizza. Sprinkle with rawmesan or nutritional yeast and red pepper flakes.

Place in dehydrator at 100°F. and dry for about one hour.

Fresh Pizza

Preparation: 30 Min. *Drying:* 1-3 Hrs. *Makes 4-6 Servings*

Ingredients

Almond Crust

- 1 c. almonds, soaked overnight
- 1 tbsp. coconut flower overnight
- ½ c. buckwheat, soaked
- ¼ c. raw tahini
- ½ tsp. Himalayan crystal salt

Creamy Topping

- ¾ c. macadamia nut
- ½ lemon, juiced
- ½ tsp. Himalayan crystal salt
- ½ c. pure water
- ¼ tsp. dill
- 1 clove garlic, crushed

Toppings

- ½ c. cauliflower, chopped
- ½ c. broccoli, chopped
- ½ c. carrot, shredded
- ½ c. red bell pepper, chopped
- ½ c. yellow bell pepper, chopped
- ½ c. raw olives, sliced

Directions

Soak almonds overnight, while skin is wet peel brown skin off.

Place almonds, coconut flour, ground buckwheat, tahini and salt in a food processor and mix until well combined.

Shape the crust. Make sure to fold up to create an edge. Place on non-stick dehydrator sheet and dry for one hour.

Remove the non-stick sheet and continue drying for 30 to 60 minutes depending on how thick the crust is. Crust should be bread consistency.

Into a blender, combine macadamia nuts, lemon juice, salt, dill, and garlic adding water as needed to achieve a creamy texture.

Spread creamy topping over the crust and top with cauliflower, broccoli, carrot, red and yellow bell pepper, and pitted raw olives

Philly Pizza

Preparation:	Soaking:	Drying:	Makes 4-6
30 Min.	8-12 Hrs.	1-3 Hrs.	Servings

Ingredients

- pizza crust (page 70)

Mushroom 'Steak'

- 3 dried Portobello mushrooms, thinly sliced
- 2 tbsp. cold pressed olive oil
- 4 tbs. grapefruit, juiced
- 2 tsp. cumin, ground
- 2 tsp. coriander, ground
- 1 tsp. rosemary, ground
- 1 tsp. celery seed, ground
- 1 tbs. raw apple cider vinegar

Vegetables

- 1 dried red bell pepper, chopped
- 1 dried yellow bell pepper, chopped
- 1 dried orange bell pepper, chopped
- 1 ½ c. dried broccoli, chopped
- 3 tbsp. onion, copped
- 1 garlic clove
- 1 tsp. Himalayan crystal salt
- 1 tsp. savory, ground
- 2 tbsp. cold pressed olive oil

Cheese

- 1 c. sunflower seeds, soaked overnight
- 1 c. pumpkin seeds, soaked overnight
- 3 tbs. raw apple cider vinegar
- ½ tsp. oregano, dried
- 2 tsp. onion
- 1 tsp. Himalayan crystal salt
- ¼ c. or more water

Directions

The 'Steak':

Slice mushrooms and place them in a bowl. Juice grapefruit in a small bowl. To the grapefruit add cumin, coriander, rosemary, ground celery seed, oil, and vinegar stir. Pour olive oil mixture over the mushrooms making sure they are well coated. Let mushrooms marinate while preparing vegetables.

Vegetables:

In a bowl, place peppers, onion, garlic, savory, and salt then mix add olive oil.

Cheese:

Soak the sunflower and pumpkin seeds overnight. Drain the water off the seeds. Place seeds in a blender and add vinegar, oregano, onion, and salt blend until smooth adding water as needed.

Putting it together:

Evenly spread half the cheese on the crust. Arrange mushrooms over cheese then place vegetables and the remaining cheese. Or mix the mushrooms and vegetable with the cheese and spread over the crust.

Jamaican Jerk Zucchini Pizza

Preparation: 15 Min. Drying: 1-3 Hrs Makes 4-6 Servings

Ingredients

- pizza crust (page 70)
- 1 ½ c. zucchini, shredded
- almond mayo (page 80)
- red bell pepper, sliced

Jerk Sauce

- 1 garlic, clove
- ½ habanero pepper
- 1 green onion
- 3 tbsp. lemon/lime, juice
- ½ tsp. thyme, dried
- ¼ tsp. allspice, ground
- ¼ tsp. cinnamon, ground
- ¼ tsp. nutmeg, ground
- black pepper to taste
- ½ tsp. parsley
- ¼ tsp. paprika
- a pinch of Himalayan crystal salt

Directions

Make pizza crust and almond mayo.

Grate zucchini and place in a bowl. Pour jerk sauce over zucchini and let marinate at least 1 hour, can be marinated overnight if desired.

Spread almond mayo over the crust in a thick layer. Layer marinated zucchini and bell pepper slices. Place in a dehydrator and dry for about an hour at 100°F.

Jerk Sauce

Remove seeds from habanero. In a blender, combine habanero, garlic, green onion, thyme, allspice, cinnamon, nutmeg, paprika, parsley, lemon/lime juice, coconut nectar, salt, and pepper blend until well mixed.

Artichoke Zucchini Pizza

Preparation: 30 Min. *Drying:* 1-3 Hrs. *Makes 4-6 Servings*

Ingredients

- 1 pizza crust (page 70)

Topping:

- 1 zucchini, thinly sliced
- 1 red or yellow bell pepper, sliced
- ½ c. sun dried olives
- ½ c. artichokes hearts (optional not a raw product)
- 1 c. nut mayo (page 80)

Sauce:

- 3 tomatoes
- 1 tbs. pizza seasoning
- 2 tbs. olive oil

Directions

Make nut mayo and set aside.

Place tomatoes, pizza seasoning, and olive oil in a blender and mix until well blended.

Wash and slice zucchini, bell peppers, and olives. Chop artichoke hearts.

Place pizza sauce on crust. Layer artichoke hearts, zucchini, bell peppers, and olives. Drop mayo over the top, for cheese.

Dry at 100°F. in a dehydrator for an hour or two.

Fun Fact:

According to Greek myth, the artichoke (Cynara cardunculus) owes its existence to Zeus who fell instantly in love with Cynara, seduced her, made her a goddess, and took her back with him to Mount Olympus. She was lonesome and missing her mother and took to sneaking home to visit her family. This duplicitous act so infuriated Zeus that—in a fit of temper he tossed Cynara from Olympus and turned her into an artichoke.

Pesto Pizza

Preparation: 45 Min. *Drying:* 1-3 Hrs.. *Makes 4-6 Servings*

Ingredients

- 1 cauliflower pizza crust (page 66)
- carrot, thinly sliced
- 2-3 tomatoes, sliced
- 3 tbsp. basil, chopped

Pesto

- ½ c. fresh spinach leaves
- ¼ c. fresh parsley
- 1 tbsp. dried basil
- 1 tbsp. dried oregano
- 1 clove garlic, minced
- 1-2 green onion
- ½ c. pumpkin seeds, soaked 3-5 hours
- ½ small zucchini, shredded
- 4 or more tbsp. cold pressed olive oil
- Himalayan crystal salt to taste
- pure water as needed

Directions

Make pizza crust.

Thinly slice carrot using a vegetable peeler. Slice tomatoes and chop basil. Spread pesto over the pizza crust. Top with carrot, tomatoes, and basil.

Pesto

Soak pumpkin seeds at least 3 hours, they can be soaked overnight, drain water off and place pumpkin seeds in food processor. To the food processor add spinach, parsley, garlic, onion, zucchini, oil, oregano, basil, green onion, zucchini, and salt puree to a semi-smooth paste adding water as needed.

Fun Fact:

Ancient Romans made something similar to pesto with different herbs, cilantro, thyme, dill, and oregano, named 'moretum'.

Pear and Gorgonzola Style Cheese Pizza

Preparation: 15 Min.   *Drying:* 60-90 Min.   *Makes 4-6 Servings*

Ingredients

- pizza crust (page 70)

Toppings

- 1 bosc pear, chopped
- 2 tbsp. walnuts, chopped
- 5 tbsp. Gorgonzola style cheese (page 84) crumbled
- 1-3 tsp. dill weed
- ½ c. almond mayo (page 80)

Directions

Make crust and cheese. Spread almond mayo over top of the crust.

Arrange pears over mayo, sprinkle with walnuts and gorgonzola cheese.

Dry at about 100°F for about 90 minutes. Top with dill. Slice and enjoy.

Blackberry Basil Pizza

Preparation: *Drying:*   *Makes 4-6*
20 Min.   30 Min.   Servings

Ingredients

- 1 pizza crust (page 70)
- 1 c. blackberries halved
- 1 c. almond lemon spread (page 73)
- ¼ c. basil leaves sliced into strips

Directions

Make pizza crust dry it for about 30 minutes at 100°F.

Prepare almond lemon spread.

Smash half of the blackberries and ½ the chopped basil and spread out over the crust.

Reserve ¼ of the lemon spread. Using remaining lemon spread cover the pizza crust.

Scatter remaining blackberries over pizza. Drop reserved lemon spread randomly over top of the pizza.

Scatter reaming basil leaves over pizza before serving.

Greek Pizza

Preparation: 20 Min. Drying: 30-90 Min. Makes 4-6 Servings

Ingredients

- pizza crust (page 70)
- ½ c. vegan feta cheese (page 89)
- ½ c. red, yellow or orange bell pepper, chopped
- 1 c. tomatoes, chopped
- ¼ c. sundried olives, sliced
- ¼ c. red onion, chopped
- 1 tbsp. basil, chopped

Greek dressing

- ¼ c. cold pressed extra-virgin olive oil
- 1 lemon, juiced
- ¼ tsp. mustard seed, ground
- ½ tsp. oregano, dried
- ½ tsp. basil, dried
- ½ tsp. garlic powder
- ¼ tsp. Himalayan crystal salt
- black pepper to taste

Directions

Prepare pizza crust and dry in dehydrator for about 30 minutes.

In a jar with a tight lid combine olive oil, lemon juice, mustard seed, oregano, basil, garlic, salt, and pepper.

Marinate bell peppers, tomatoes, olives, and onion in dressing for about 10 minutes.

Brush crust evenly with olive oil mixture. Top with vegetables, basil, and vegan feta.

Fun Fact:

Traditional Greek pizza is a style of pizza crust and how it is prepared. It is baked in a pan heavily oiled with olive oil. This pizza gets its name from the topping and the lightly oiled pizza crust.

Brussels Sprout Pizza

Preparation: 20 Min.   *Drying:* 1-3 Hrs.   *Makes 4-6 Servings*

Ingredients

- pizza crust (page 70)
- 1 c. Brussels sprouts
- 1 pinch cayenne
- 1 tsp. Himalayan crystal salt to taste
- black pepper to taste
- 2 tsp. cold pressed olive oil
- 1 tbsp. coconut vinegar or raw apple cider vinegar
- 1 tbsp. pizza seasoning
- ¼ c. red onion
- ¼ c. yellow or red bell pepper, chopped
- 1 ½ c. almond mayo (page 80)
- ¼ c. rasmesan cheese (page 83)

Directions

Make pizza crust and shape on a nonstick dehydrator sheet. Dry in the dehydrator for about 30 min. at 100°F.

Use a mandolin and thinly slice Brussels sprouts and red onion. Chop bell pepper and place in a bowl with Brussels sprouts and onion, add olive oil, salt, pepper, cayenne pepper, pizza seasoning, and vinegar then toss. Let marinate for at least 2 hours.

Spread almond mayo over the pizza crust. Spread Brussels sprout mix over the mayo. Sprinkle with rawmesan cheese. Dry in dehydrator about an hour.

Fun Fact:

Brussels sprouts were very popular in 16th century Belgium and were named after the capital Brussels. They have 26 calories a cup and one ounce contains 5 grams of fiber and 5 grams of protein. One serving has four times the amount of vitamin c of an orange.

Taco Pizza

Preparation: 20 Min. *Drying:* 1-2 Hrs. *Makes 4-6 Servings*

Ingredients

- corn pizza crust (page 71)

Toppings

- lettuce, shredded (optional)
- avocado, sliced
- spicy cheese (page 82)
- almond sour cream (page 79)
- ½ c. olives, sliced

Salsa

- 1 yellow bell pepper, chopped
- 1 orange or red bell pepper, chopped
- 1 hot peppers, chopped
- ¼ c. onion, chopped
- 1 c. fresh tomatoes, chopped
- 1 cloves garlic, minced
- 1 tbsp. fresh cilantro, chopped
- 1 lime, juiced

Directions

Prepare corn pizza crust, almond sour cream, and spicy cheese.

Salsa

Wash and chop yellow bell pepper, orange bell pepper, hot pepper, onion, tomatoes, garlic, and cilantro then combine in a bowl along with lime juice.

This can be done in a food processor and pulse but be careful because it can turn into soup easily.

Putting the pizza together

Spread spicy cheese over the pizza crust. Spread salsa over cheese then sprinkle with olives May warm in the dehydrator for about 2 hours at 100°F.

Scatter lettuce, avocado, and tomatoes on top of pizza then drop almond sour cream randomly over the pizza just before serving.

Lemon Pizza

Preparation: 20 Min.   *Drying:* 30 Min   *Makes 4-6 Servings*

Ingredients

- 1 pizza crust (page 70)
- almond lemon spread (page 73)
- 1 tsp. Italian seasoning
- ¼ tsp. Himalayan crystal salt
- 1 zucchini, sliced
- 1 small lemon, halved, thinly sliced, seeds removed
- 2 tbsp. chives, chopped
- ¼-½ poppy seeds
- basil for garnish (optional)

Directions

Make pizza crust and dry in the dehydrator for about an30 min. at 100°F.

Very thinly slice the zucchini and lemon into rounds.

Top pizza evenly with almond lemon spread, then evenly scatter zucchini and lemon pieces over top. Sprinkle the surface of pizza with a little salt.

Dry in the dehydrator for about 1 hour at 100°F. Finish pizza with a sprinkling of chives, poppy seeds, and basil.

Veggie Ranch Pizza

Preparation:	Drying:	Makes 4-6
30 Min.	1-3 Hrs.	Servings

Ingredients

- 1 pizza crust (page 70)
- ½ c. carrots, shredded
- ½ c. cauliflower, chopped
- ½ c. fresh broccoli, chopped
- ½ c. onion, chopped
- ½ c. red bell pepper, chopped
- ½ c. fresh mushrooms, sliced
- 2 c. sour cream (page 79)
- 2 tbs. green onion, finely chopped
- 2 tsp. parsley, minced
- 2 tsp. celery seed
- ¼ tsp. garlic powder
- ¼ tsp. onion powder
- ¼ tsp. paprika
- pinch cayenne pepper
- ¼ tsp. Himalayan crystal salt
- ¼ tsp. black pepper

Directions

In a small bowl combine almond sour cream, green onion, parsley, celery seed, garlic, onion, paprika, cayenne pepper, salt, and pepper then mix well.

Spread sour cream mixture evenly over top of the crust. Sprinkle carrots, cauliflower, broccoli, onion, red pepper, and mushrooms over the pizza.

Dry at about 100°F for about 1-3 hours.

Fun Fact:

While cooking for his construction crew in Anchorage, Alaska, Steve Henson played around with a buttermilk dressing recipe until he found the perfect combination of garlic, onion and fresh herbs. Later he sold his ranch dressing recipe for $8 million.

Tomato and Basil Pizza

Preparation: 40 Min. *Drying:* 1-3 Hrs. *Makes 4-6 Servings*

Ingredients

- cauliflower pizza crust (page 66)
- ½ c. cherry tomatoes
- ½ c. basil leaves

Cheese sauce:

- ½ c. cashews
- ¼ c. pumpkin seeds
- 1 tbsp. nutritional yeast (optional)
- 1 tbsp. raw apple cider vinegar
- ½ tsp. Himalayan crystal salt
- ¼ tsp. garlic powder

Marinara sauce

- 1 clove garlic
- ½ c. dried tomatoes
- 1 c. fresh tomatoes
- 1 tsp. red pepper flakes
- 1 tsp. oregano
- 1 tsp. Himalayan crystal salt
- black pepper

Directions

The Marinara sauce:

Soak dried tomatoes in pure water for about 30 minutes.

Place soaked tomatoes in a blender with fresh tomatoes, red pepper flakes, garlic, oregano, salt, and pepper and mix until well blended. Add tomato soaking water to thin if desired.

The Cheese Sauce:

Soak pumpkin seeds overnight. Drain off the water and place seeds in a blender.

Add cashews to the blender with nutritional yeast, raw apple cider vinegar, garlic powder, salt, and pepper and mix until well combined. Add water if needed to achieve a creamy mixture.

The Pizza:

Spread marinara sauce over cauliflower crust. Top with cheese sauce, tomatoes, and chopped basil.

Green Pizza

Preparation: 30 Min.   *Drying:* 1-3 Hrs.   Makes 4-6 Servings

Ingredients

- pizza crust (page 70)
- ½ c. pistachios, shelled
- 1 ½ c. fresh basil
- 1 clove garlic, minced
- 1 tbsp. cold pressed olive oil
- 1 ½ tbsp. lemon, juiced
- ½ tsp. Himalayan crystal salt
- 1 tsp. lemon zest (optional)
- ½ c. zucchini, shredded (optional)
- ½ c. basic seed cheese (page 88)
- ¼ c. leek, finely chopped
- ½ c. broccoli, chopped
- ½ c. micro green sprouts

Directions

Make pizza crust and set aside.

Place pistachios, basil, garlic, lemon juice, lemon zest, zucchini, olive oil, and salt in a food processor and puree to a semi-smooth paste. Add water as needed. Spread on crust.

In a bowl mix basic seed cheese, broccoli, and leek Mix making sure the broccoli is very well coated. Place on dehydrator trays and dry and 115°F. for about 4-6 hours or until broccoli is soft. Spread broccoli mix on top of pizza. Dry for about 2 hours. Sprinkle with green sprouts just before serving.

Hummus Pizza

Preparation: 30 Min.   Drying: 1-3 Hrs.   Makes 4-6 Servings

Ingredients

- pizza crust (page70)
- 1 c. hummus (page 73)
- ¾ tsp. oregano, dried
- ¼ tsp. crushed red pepper flakes (optional)
- ½ c. vegan feta cheese (page 89)
- ½ c. tomatoes, soaked
- ½ c. sundried olives, chopped

Directions

Prepare crust and hummus set aside.

In a small bowl, mix hummus, oregano, and red pepper flakes then spread over crust.

Sprinkle feta cheese, tomatoes, and olives over hummus.

Pizza Appetizer

Preparation: 20 Min.   Makes 6-8 Servings

Ingredients

- 16 mushrooms caps
- 5 cherry tomatoes, sliced
- ½ c. herbed cream cheese (page 87)
- 8 slices of Nadhirrah's baykon (page 76)

Directions

Place mushroom caps upside down on a platter (the stem ends up) stuff herbed cream cheese inside the mushroom cap. Top with a slice of tomato and half a strip of bacon just before serving.

Note

Try using pizza seasoning when making herbed cream cheese.

BBQ Pizza

Preparation: 40 Min. *Drying:* 1-3 Hrs. *Makes 4-6 Servings*

Ingredients

- pizza crust (page 70)
- ½ head of cauliflower
- 1 tsp. paprika

BBQ Sauce

- 1 c. water
- ½ c. dried tomatoes
- 1 date, pitted (optional)
- 1 garlic clove
- 1 tsp. raw apple cider vinegar
- 1 tsp. chili powder
- 1 tsp. mustard seed, ground
- ½ tsp. cayenne pepper
- ½ tsp. celery seed
- ¼ tsp. Himalayan crystal salt

Garlic Sauce

- ½ c. cashews
- 2 garlic cloves
- Himalayan crystal salt to taste
- black pepper to taste

Directions

Cut cauliflower into bite-sized florets. Combine BBQ sauce with paprika. Marinate cauliflower in BBQ sauce, be sure they are completely coated, for at least an hour or overnight if desired.

Make crust and dry halfway through, about 30 min. at 100°F. On crust, thinly spread ¼ cup BBQ sauce. Place marinated cauliflower over crust and place in dehydrator for 2-4 hours. Sprinkle with chopped parsley and green onions. Drizzle garlic sauce over top and serve.

BBQ Sauce

Soak dried tomatoes and date in water for about an hour. Place the tomatoes and date in a blender with mustard seed, cayenne pepper, celery seed, chili powder, vinegar, salt, and garlic puree until a smooth consistency is reached adding soaking water as needed.

Garlic Sauce

In blender, combine cashews, garlic, salt, and pepper until smooth adding water as needed. It should be smooth and on the thin side but not watery.

Spicy Brazil Nut Zausage Pizza

Preparation: 45 Min. *Drying: 1-3 Hrs.* *Makes 4-6 Servings*

Ingredients

- 1 pizza crust (page 70)
- ¼ c. mini sweet peppers, thinly sliced
- 1 c. vegan feta cheese (page 89)
- 1 tablespoon crushed red pepper

Spicy Brazil Nut Sausage

- ½ c. Brazil nuts, soaked
- ¼ c. onion, thinly sliced
- 1 tbsp. coconut aminos
- 1 tbsp. jalapeno pepper
- ¼ c. tomatoes, chopped
- ½ tsp. cumin
- 1 clove garlic
- 1 tbsp. nutritional yeast (optional)
- ¼ tsp. Himalayan crystal salt
- ¼ tsp. thyme
- ¼ tsp. sage
- ¼ tsp. rosemary
- ¼ tsp. cayenne pepper
- ¼ tsp. paprika
- ½ - ¾ c. water

Marinara sauce

- 1 clove garlic
- ¼ c. dried tomatoes
- ½ c. fresh tomatoes
- ½ tsp. red pepper flakes (optional)
- ½ tsp. oregano
- ½ tsp. Himalayan crystal salt
- black pepper

Directions

Spicy Brazil Nut Zausage

Soak brazil nuts overnight. Drain the water off.

Soak dried tomatoes for about 20 minutes in pure water. Remove tomatoes but save tomato soaking water for use later.

Place brazil nuts in a food processor, add onion, soaked tomatoes, garlic, cumin, coconut aminos, salt, thyme, sage, rosemary, cayenne pepper, paprika, jalapeno pepper, and nutritional yeast pulse until looks mixed and crumbly. If too dry add tomato soaking water. Set aside.

The Marinara sauce:

Soak dried tomatoes in pure water for about 30 minutes. Remove from water and place the soaked tomatoes in a blender with fresh tomatoes, red pepper flakes, garlic, oregano, salt, and pepper and mix until well blended.

Putting the pizza together

Make pizza crust and shape it into a 12-inch circle.

Spread marinara sauce evenly over the crust. Randomly drop feta cheese over pizza and sprinkle zausage and peppers over the sauce.

Zuccheroni Pizza

Preparation: 40 Min. *Drying:* 1-3 Hrs. *Makes 4-6 Servings*

Ingredients

- pizza crust (page 70)
- almond mayo (page 80)

Zuccheroni

- 1 zucchini
- ½ tsp. paprika
- ½ tsp. garlic powder
- ½ tsp. Himalayan crystal salt
- ½ tsp. mustard seed, ground
- ½ tsp. cayenne powder
- ¼ tsp. black pepper
- ¼ tsp. anise seed, ground
- 1 tsp. coconut aminos
- ½ tsp. coconut nectar
- 2 tbsp. cold pressed olive oil

Pizza Sauce

- ¼ c. dried tomatoes, soaked
- ½ c. fresh tomatoes
- 1 tsp. cold pressed olive oil
- ½ tsp. oregano
- ½ tsp. thyme
- 1 clove garlic
- Himalayan crystal salt to taste
- black pepper to taste

Directions

Zuccheroni

Thinly slice zucchini into rounds.

In a bowl, mix paprika, garlic powder, salt, mustard seed, cayenne powder, black pepper, anise seed, coconut amino, coconut nectar, and olive oil.

Add zucchini to the spice mix and gently toss make sure zucchinis are well covered. Set aside and let 'cure' in the refrigerator for 2 or more hours.

Lay zucchini rounds on dehydrator try in a single layer and dry for about an hour.

Pizza Sauce

Soak dried tomatoes in water for 30 minutes. Drain water off tomatoes but save soaking water. Place soaked tomatoes in a blender with fresh tomatoes, olive oil, oregano, thyme, garlic, salt, and pepper blend until smooth.

Putting it together

Prepare pizza crust and almond mayo.

Spread pizza sauce over crust. drop mayo over the top. Layer zuccheroni over mayo and dry the pizza in a dehydrator for an hour or two at 100°F.

Place chopped red, orange, and yellow bell pepper over pizza.

Jalapeno Popper Pizza

Preparation: 25 Min.   *Drying:* 1-3 Hrs.   *Makes 4-6 Servings*

Ingredients

- corn pizza crust (page 71)
- ½ c. tomatoes, sliced
- 1 avocado, chopped
- rawmesan (page 83)
- ¼ c. almond sour cream (page 79)
- 1 ½ c. jalapenos
- ¼ c. cashews
- ¼ c. pumpkins seed soaked overnight
- 1 lemon, juiced
- ½ tsp. Himalayan crystal salt
- 1 tsp. dried dill or a little more fresh
- 1 green onion, chopped
- ½ c. red bell pepper
- ½ c. tomato, chopped
- 1 clove garlic
- ¼ c. pure water or more as needed
- ½ tsp. cumin, ground
- ½ tsp. paprika
- ½ tsp. oregano
- ½ tsp. basil, dried or 4-5 fresh leaves

Directions

Soak pumpkins seeds overnight, drain water off.

In a blender, combine soaked pumpkin seeds, cashews, lemon juice, salt, dill, cumin, paprika, oregano, basil, green onions, bell pepper, and tomato until well mixed. Adding fresh water as needed to achieve a thick cream mixture. This is your cheese and let sit overnight.

Thinly slice jalapenos.

Spread cheese sauce over the pizza crust. Arrange sliced jalapenos mixture over the cheese.

Dry in dehydrator for about 2 hours at 100°F. Remove pizza and scatter tomatoes and avocado over top. Drizzle sour cream over the top. Sprinkle with rawmesan or nutritional yeast.

Spinach - Kohlrabi Pizza

Preparation: 30 Min. Drying: 1-3 Hrs. Makes 4-6 Servings

Ingredients

- kolrohbi pizza crust (page 67)

Cheese Sauce

- ½ c. cashews
- 1 ½ tbsp. shallots
- ½ tsp. Himalayan crystal salt
- 1 lemon, juiced
- 3 tbsp. basil
- water if needed

Toppings

- tomatoes, sliced
- basil, chopped

Directions

Make pizza crust and completely dry.

Cheese Sauce

Place cashews, shallots, salt, lemon juice and basil in a blender and mix until well combined.

Putting it together

Spread cheese sauce over the pizza crust. Top with tomatoes and basil and serve.

Fun Fact:

Kohlrabi belongs to the cabbage family. In the 19th century kohlrabi was introduced to North America.

Kohlrabi has two main varieties white (light-green) and purple. All varieties have a creamy-white flesh regardless of the color skin.

Olive Pizza on Zucchini Carrot Crust

Preparation: 20 Min.   Drying: 1-3 Hrs.   Makes 4-6 Servings

Ingredients

- 1 zucchini carrot crust (page 69)
- ½ c. olives, sliced
- 1 red, orange, or yellow bell peppers, chopped
- 1 tomatoes, sliced
- ¼ c. almond mayo (page 80)

Directions

Make zucchini carrot pizza crust.

Spread almond mayo over the pizza crust. Top with sliced tomatoes, chopped bell pepper and olives.

Easy Vegetable Pizza

Preparation: 15 Min. *Drying: 1-3 Hrs.* *Makes 4-6 Servings*

Ingredients

- pizza crust (page 70)
- 1 tsp. cold pressed olive oil
- 1 garlic clove, minced
- ¼ c. onion, finely chopped
- ½ c. broccoli, shredded
- ½ c. carrot, shredded
- ½ c. zucchini, shredded
- ½ c. almond mayo (page 80)
- 2 tbsp. rawmesan (page 83)

Directions

Prepare pizza crust. Dry about 30 min. at 100°F.

Spread almond mayo over the crust.

In a bowl mix shredded broccoli, carrot, zucchini, onion, garlic and toss with olive oil, salt, and pepper. Spread over the pizza.

Sprinkle with rawmesan.

Fun Fact:

Onions are one of the oldest foods known, the oldest know cultivation of onion dates back to around 5,000 BCE. They are so old they are even mentioned in the Bible as one of the foods the Israelites ate. Ancient Egyptians even worshipped the onion. They believed that concentric rings and spherical shape of the onions were symbols of eternity.

The Romans took onions to Europe when they made their way across the continent and the Pilgrims brought onions to the US when they came over on the Mayflower.

Meet-za Pizza

Preparation: 65 Min.   *Drying: 4-6 Hrs.*   *Makes 4-6 Servings*

Ingredients

- ½ c. basic seed cheese (page 88)
- ¼ c. sundried olives, sliced
- ¼ c. fresh basil, chopped
- ¼ c. tomatoes, sliced

Brazil nut Crust

- ½ c. Brazil nuts, soaked
- 1 ½ c. zucchini, shredded
- 1 tbsp. onion, diced
- ¼ c. walnuts
- 1 garlic clove
- 1 ½ tsp. Himalayan crystal salt
- 1 tsp. poultry seasoning
- ¼ tsp. black pepper
- ¼ c. red bell pepper, chopped
- ¼ c. celery, chopped
- 1 tbsp. cold pressed olive oil
- 1 tbsp. psyllium husk powder or flax seed, ground in coffee grinder
- ½-1 c. water

Filling

- 2 tbs. Italian seasoning
- 1 garlic clove
- ½ c. dried tomatoes
- ¼ c. onion, diced
- ½ c. red bell pepper, diced
- 1 c. fresh tomatoes
- 1 ½ tsp. cold pressed olive oil
- Himalayan crystal salt to taste
- black pepper to taste
- ¼ c water

Directions

Filling

Soak dried tomatoes water for 15 minutes. Place soaked tomatoes and water in blender with, Italian seasoning, garlic, ¼ c. onion, ½ c. red bell pepper, fresh tomatoes, olive oil, salt, and pepper and combine until smooth.

Pour blender mixture in a bowl and add reaming onion and bell peppers. For best results let filling marinate overnight.

Crust

Soak Brazil nuts and walnuts overnight. Drain off water and place the nuts in a food processor.

In a small bowl place grown flax seed and 3 tablespoons water and let sit for 10 minutes.

To the food processor add zucchini, celery, red bell pepper, onion, garlic, poultry seasoning, pepper, psyllium husk, flax seeds, olive oil, salt, and pepper combine until well mixed. Should have meatloaf texture.

Shape crust into a pizza size round. Fold up the edge so pizza will hold filling. Place in dehydrator on nonstick sheet for about 2 hours.

Putting it together

Remove the nonstick sheet from bottom and replace crust on dehydrator tray. Into the center of the crust place tomato filling. Place basic seed cheese in large dollops and place into dehydrator and continue drying 2-4 hours at 100°F.

Sprinkle olives, tomatoes, and basil over the top just before serving.

Avocado Pizza

Preparation: 45 Min. *Makes 4-6 Servings*

Ingredients

- corn pizza crust (page 71)
- ¾ c. fresh corn kernels
- 1 c. tomato, chopped
- ½ c. avocado, cubed
- ¼ c. basil, chopped
- ¼ c. red or orange bell pepper, chopped
- 2 tbsp. sundried olives, chopped
- ½ lemon, juiced
- 2 tsp. Italian seasoning
- 1 tsp. cumin, ground
- ½ tsp. Himalayan crystal salt
- ¼ tsp. black pepper

Avocado Pesto

- ½ c. nut mayo (page 80)
- 1 green onion, chopped
- 1 avocado, if small you may need more
- ¼ lemon, juiced
- Himalayan crystal salt to taste
- black pepper to taste

Directions

Make pizza crust and nut mayo.

Avocado Pesto

In a bowl, place peeled and pitted avocado mash with a fork. To avocado add mayo, green onion, garlic, lemon juice, salt, and pepper and mix well. Spread over crust.

Putting Pizza Together

Remove kernels from fresh corn and place in a bowl. To the bowl add tomato, basil, bell pepper, avocado, Italian seasoning, cumin, salt, and pepper mix well then spread over crust.

Fun Fact:

The Mayans reserved avocados for royal tables of luxury. It was said that a Mayan princess ate the first avocado.

Carrot Tops Herb Pizza

Preparation: 20 Min. Drying: 1-3 Hrs. Makes 4-6 Servings

Ingredients

- pizza crust (page 70)
- ¼ c. rawmesan (page 83)
- 1 garlic clove, grated
- 1 tbsp. fresh lime juice
- ¾ c. basil
- ¾ c. carrot top (green leaf part)
- ½ c. mint leaves
- Himalayan crystal salt to taste
- 1 tbsp. cold pressed olive oil
- 1 c. carrots, finely sliced
- ¼ c. pea greens or other micro greens (optional)

Directions

Make pizza crust and set aside.

In a blender, combine rawmesan, garlic, lime juice, ½ c. basil, ½ c. carrot tops, ½ c. mint leaves, salt, and olive oil until well mixed adding water if needed to achieve a smooth paste. Spread over pizza crust.

Use a mandolin to thinly slice carrots. Place carrot slices over pesto. Place in dehydrator for about an hour.

Top with reserved carrot tops, basil, mint, pea greens or other micro green and serve immediately.

Fun Fact:

Carrot tops have a peppery flavor, similar to arugula or parsley and can bring that same sort of spice to a range of dishes. When cooking with them, remove the fibrous stems, as you would any other tender herb such as parsley or dill. They contain 6 times the vitamin C of the root and are a great source of potassium and calcium.

Bonce Tip:

Carrot leaves have antiseptic qualities and can be juiced and used as a mouthwash.

Apple Pie Pizza

Preparation: 20- Min. *Drying: 1-3 Hrs.* *Makes 4-6 Servings*

Ingredients

- 1 sweet pizza crust (page 72)
- vanilla or banana ice cream, (optional)

Apple Topping

- 4 medium apples
- 1 tsp. ground cinnamon
- ½ c. coconut sugar

Date Carmel

- 1 c. pitted dates
- water to thin
- pinch Himalayan crystal salt

Crisp Topping

- ¼ c. almonds
- 2 tbsp. coconut sugar
- ¼ c. coconut, shredded
- 1 tsp. cinnamon

Directions

Make sweet crust and dry completely.

Apple Topping

Peel and cut apples into ½-inch slices.

Combine sugar, flour, and cinnamon in a bowl. Add apple slices to sugar mixture and toss.

Arrange apples in a single layer in a circular pattern to completely cover the crust.

Crisp Topping

In food processor, combine almonds, coconut sugar, and cinnamon, mixt until well mixed but still crumbly, sprinkle over the apples

Date Caramel

If the dates are not moist and sticky, soak them in water for 10 minutes, drain and save the water.

Place the dates and salt in a food processor and pulse. Scrape down the sides periodically. Add only enough date soaking water to form a paste. The amount will depend on your machine and size and moistness of dates.

Drizzle with the date caramel and sprinkle with coconut. Serve with ice cream if desired.

Coconut Berry Pizza

Preparation: 15 Min. Drying: 1-3 Hrs. Makes 4-6 Servings

Ingredients

- sweet pizza crust (page 72)
- 1 c. fruit cream cheese (page 86)
- 4 medium kiwifruits, peeled and sliced
- 1 ¼ c. strawberries, sliced
- 1 ¼ c. raspberries
- 1 ¼ c. blueberries
- 1 ¼ c. blackberries
- ½ c. shredded coconut

Directions

Prepare sweet pizza crust and dry it completely, about 2 hours at 100°F.

Make fruit cream cheese using dried shredded coconut and mix until smooth. Spread over crust.

Arrange fruit over top. Sprinkle with coconut. Chill until serving

Fun Fact:

The majority of the one million tons of kiwifruit is produced in Italy, New Zealand and Chile. Kiwi is botanically a berry.

It has brown fuzzy skin and bright green or yellow flesh with a circle of dark seed in the middle. The taste and texture of the fruit depends on the species.

Kiwi is usually consumed raw or in juices. High cooking temperatures change the taste and color of Kiwi.

Kiwifruit has a high vitamin C level. Kiwi also boosts immune systems and facilitates food digestion.

Brownie Pizza

Preparation: 20 Min. *Drying: 1-3 Hrs.* *Makes 4-6 Servings*

Ingredients

- ½ c. almonds, sliced
- ½ c. almond butter
- 1 c. strawberries, sliced

Chocolate Sauce

- ¼ c. raw carob powder
- 3 tbsp. raw coconut nectar
- 1 tsp. pure vanilla extract
- Water as needed

Brownie Crust

- ½ c. carrots, shredded
- 1 c. walnuts, soaked
- ½ c. cashews
- ½ c. dates,
- ¼ tsp. Himalayan crystal salt
- 1 tsp. cinnamon
- ½ c. raw carob powder
- ½ tsp. vanilla extract
- pinch of cayenne powder

Cream Cheese Topping

- ½ c. cashews
- ½ c. water
- 2 tbsp. coconut nectar
- 1 tbsp. pure vanilla
- ¼ tsp. Himalayan crystal salt
- 1 c. unsweetened coconut flakes

Directions

Brownie Crust

Soak walnuts overnight. Drain water off and place walnuts in food processor with carrots, cashews, and dates. Combine until they are well mixed. Add salt, cinnamon, carob, coconut oil, and vanilla to the food possessor mix until they are incorporated. Shape pizza crust about ½ inch thick and place on a nonstick dehydrator sheet on a tray. Dehydrate about 4 hours then flip, remove the nonstick sheet.

Coconut Cream Cheese

In a blender, combine cashews water, coconut oil, coconut nectar, vanilla, and salt. Blend until smooth. Mix in coconut flakes. Spread over the crust.

Chocolate Sauce

In a bowl, combine carob, coconut nectar, and vanilla. Adding water as needed to achieve a thin sauce.

Putting pizza together

Spread almond butter over the crust. Mash ½ c. strawberries adding a little cream topping and spread over almond butter. Place sliced strawberries over the top. Drizzle with chocolate sauce and cream cheese topping. Sprinkle with sliced almonds.

Fruit Pizza

| Preparation: | Soaking: | Drying: | Makes 4-6 |
| 15 Min. | 6-8 Hrs. | 1-2 Hrs. | Servings |

Ingredients

- 1 sweet crust (page 72)

Glaze

- 1 ripe banana
- 1 tsp. ginger
- ¼ c. pineapple juice or orange juice
- 1 tsp. lemon, juiced

Fruit Toppings

- 2 c. strawberries
- 1 c. blueberries
- 1 ¼ c. mandarin oranges

Cream Cheese Topping

- ¾ c. cashews
- ¼ c. water
- 1 tbsp. coconut nectar
- 2 tsp. pure vanilla
- ¼ tsp. Himalayan crystal salt

Directions

Make sweet pizza crust. Dry in dehydrator for about 1-2 hours at 100°F.

Glaze

In a blender, combine banana, ginseng, pineapple juice, and lemon juice mix until smooth.

Cream Cheese Topping

In a blender, combine cashews, water, coconut oil, coconut nectar, vanilla, and salt. Blend until smooth.

Fruit Topping

Wash and cut strawberries in half. Peel and segment mandarin oranges. Wash blueberries and place in a bowl with strawberries and oranges. Gently coat fruit with glaze. Remove fruit from glaze.

Putting it together

Spread cream cheese over crust. Arrange berries and orange slices. Refrigerate until cold.

Fun Fact:

The first explorers thought a pineapple resembled a pine cone and it came to be known as "Pine of the Indies". "Apple" was added by the English to associate it with juicy delectable fruits.

Dragon Pizza

Preparation: *Drying:*   *Makes 4-6*
25 Min.   *1-3 Hrs.*   *Servings*

Ingredients

Ginger Crust

- 1 ½ c. buckwheat
- ¾ c. gold flax seeds, ground in coffee grinder
- 1 tbsp. ginger, grated
- 2 tbsp. coconut nectar
- 1 tsp. Himalayan crystal salt
- ½ c. raw coconut flour

Lemon pudding

- 1 c. macadamia nuts
- 1 young coconut meat
- ½ c. coconut water
- 1 tbsp. coconut nectar
- 2 tsp. vanilla
- 1 lemon, zest
- 1 lemon, juiced
- pinch of salt

Toppings

- ½ c. strawberries, sliced
- ½ c. green kiwi, sliced
- ½ c. yellow kiwi, sliced
- ¼ c. dragon fruit, chopped
- ½ lime, juiced

Directions

Ginger Crust

    Soak 1 cup buckwheat overnight. Drain the water off buckwheat.

    In a food processor, combine soaked buckwheat, ground flax, grated ginger, coconut nectar, and salt. Mix until a thick dough is formed.

    Using a coffee grinder, grind ½ cup of dry buckwheat to make buckwheat flour.

Use buckwheat flour to thicken the dough if it is too sticky.

Sprinkle coconut flour on the counter. Knead the dough using more coconut flour if needed until dough is soft and pliable.

Form into pizza crust and place on dehydrator try and dry about 1 hour at 100°F.

Lemon Pudding

In a blender combine macadamia nuts, young coconut meat, coconut water, coconut nectar, vanilla, salt, lemon zest and lemon juice until creamy.

Putting Pizza Together

Place lemon pudding on ginger curst.

Prepare green and yellow skin kiwi, dragon fruit, and strawberries layer over the lemon pudding.

Cinnamon Roll Pizza

Preparation: 15 Min. Drying: 3-6 Hrs. Makes 4-6 Servings

Ingredients

Crust:

- 2 c. almond pulp, left from making almond milk
- 1 c. dates, pitted and soaked

Cinnamon Topping:

- ½ c. walnuts or pecans, soaked
- 1 ½ tbsp. cinnamon, ground
- 1 c. raisins
- ½ c. raw coconut sugar
- 2 tbsp. cold pressed olive oil
- ½ tsp. turmeric
- 1 tsp. Himalayan crystal salt
- ½ inch vanilla bean or ½ tbsp. vanilla extract

Creamy Glaze:

- ½ c. macadamia nut
- ½ c. cashews
- ½ c. raw coconut nectar
- 1 lemon, juiced
- ½ tbsp. coconut oil
- water as needed

Directions

Crust

Soak dates in water for about 20 minutes, save soaking water for later use. In a food processor, combine almond pulp and dates until well mixed. Add date water as needed. Form dough into a round, about ¼ - ½ thick, and place in dehydrator for about 2 hours at 100°F.

Cinnamon Topping

In a small container, mix olive oil, turmeric, and salt then brush over crust. In a food processor, coarsely chop walnuts or pecans then place in a bowl. To the bowl add cinnamon, raisins, vanilla, and coconut sugar mix well. Evenly spread mixture over the crust pressing down to push topping into crust. Place in dehydrator for about 2 more hours at 100°F.

Creamy Glaze

Soak cashews and macadamia nuts for 10 minutes. Drain off water and place nuts into a blender. To the blender add lemon juice, coconut nectar, and coconut oil then blend until a smooth and creamy adding water as needed to achieve the desired texture. Drizzle glaze over the pizza before serving.

Mint Chocolate Pudding Pizza

Preparation: 15 Min. Drying: 3-6 Hrs. Makes 4-6 Servings

Ingredients

- ½ c. plain vegan cream cheese (page 86)
- ½ c. cashew cream (page 81)
- 1 raw chocolate bar (optional)

Cookie Crust

- ¾ c. almond pulp, left from making milk
- ¼ c. dates
- ¼ c. creamy almond butter
- 1 inch vanilla bean or 1 tbsp. vanilla extract
- pinch of Himalayan crystal salt

Chocolate Pudding

- 3 ripe avocadoes
- ¾ c. raw liquid sweetener
- 1 c. raw carob powder
- 3 tbsp. mint leaves 1 tsp. pure mint extract

Directions

Cookie Crust

In a food processor, combine almond pulp, dates, almond butter, vanilla, and salt mix until a thick dough is formed. If too thin add water if too thick add raw coconut flour or buckwheat flour. Form into a round and place in dehydrator for about 4 hours at 100° F.

Chocolate Pudding

In a blender, place avocadoes that have been peeled and pitted, raw coconut nectar, and mint. Blend until creamy smooth adding a little bit of water as needed for it to be creamy. You want it to be thick like pudding.

Putting It Together

On cookie crust spread plain vegan cream cheese. Layer chocolate pudding over cream cheese. Refrigerate until set about 20 minutes.

Spread cashew cream over top. Shave raw chocolate bar and sprinkle over top.

Cauliflower Pizza Crust

Preparation: *Drying:*   *Makes 4-6*
15 Min.   30-60 Min.   *Servings*

Ingredients

- 1 ½ c. buckwheat
- ¾ c. gold flax seeds, ground in coffee grinder
- 1 clove garlic
- 1 tsp. basil
- 1 tsp. oregano
- 1 tsp. Himalayan crystal salt
- ½ c. cauliflower
- ½ c. raw coconut flour

Directions

Soak 1 cup buckwheat overnight. Drain the water off buckwheat.

In a food processor, combine soaked buckwheat, ground flax, cauliflower, garlic, basil, oregano, and salt. Mix until a thick dough is formed.

Using a coffee grinder, grind ½ cup of dry buckwheat. This is now buckwheat flour.

Use buckwheat flour to thicken the dough if it is too sticky in the food processor.

Sprinkle coconut flour on the counter. Knead dough using more coconut flour if needed until the dough is soft and pliable.

Form into pizza crust and place on dehydrator try and dry 30-60 minutes at 100°F.

Note

May use buckwheat flour instead of coconut if desired. The coconut flour helps make a lighter crust.

Fun Fact:

Many people who don't like the taste of white cauliflower find they like the sweeter and milder taste of orange cauliflower.

Kohlrabi Pizza Crust

Preparation: 15 Min.   Drying: 30-60 Min.   Makes 4-6 Servings

Ingredients

- ¾ c. flax seed, ground in a coffee grinder
- 1 ¾ c. buckwheat
- 1 c. kohlrabi, shredded
- 1 tsp. Himalayan crystal salt
- 1 tbsp. shallot, chopped
- ¾ c. zucchini, shredded
- 1 c. spinach
- ½ - 2 c. raw coconut flour

Directions

Soak 1 cup buckwheat in water overnight. Drain off water.

Place soaked buckwheat, salt, ground flax seed, shallot, zucchini, and spinach in a food processor and mix.

Grind dried buckwheat in a coffee grinder and add buckwheat flour until mixture forms a dough.

Remove dough from food processor and place on a counter with raw coconut or buckwheat flour and kneed the flour into the dough until dough is soft and pliable.

Form into pizza crust and place on dehydrator tray and dry for 30-60 minutes at 100°F.

Fun Fact:

Kohlrabi is derived from the German word for cabbage (kohl) and turnip (rabi). Kohlrabi is a vegetable related to kale, cabbage and broccoli. It grows in green or purple varieties and has a white flesh. Both the bulb and the leaves can be eaten. Kohlrabi tastes somewhat like a cross between a cucumber and mild broccoli. It has a light flavor and a juicy, crisp flesh similar to an apple.

Kale Pizza Crust

Preparation: *Drying:*   *Makes 4-6*
20 Min.   30-60 Min.   *Servings*

Ingredients

- 1 ½ c. buckwheat
- ¾ c. gold flax seeds, ground in coffee grinder
- 1 tsp. Himalayan crystal salt
- ½ c. kale
- ½ c. raw coconut flour

Directions

Soak 1 cup buckwheat overnight. Drain the water off buckwheat.

In a food processor, combine soaked buckwheat, ground flax, kale with steams removed and salt. Mix until a thick dough is formed.

Using a coffee grinder, grind ½ cup of dry buckwheat. This is now buckwheat flour.

Use buckwheat flour to thicken the dough if it is too sticky in the food processor.

Sprinkle coconut flour on the counter. Knead the dough using more coconut flour if needed until the dough is soft and pliable.

Form into pizza crust and place on dehydrator try and dry 30-60 minutes at 100°F.

Note

You may use buckwheat flour instead of coconut if desired. The coconut flour helps make a lighter crust.

Fun Fact:

Kale used to be called peasant's cabbage. Today it is more like a superstar's cabbage.

Zucchini Carrot Pizza Crust

Preparation: 20 Min. *Drying: 30-60 Min.* *Makes 4-6 Servings*

Ingredients

- 1 tbsp. chia or flaxseed, ground in coffee grinder
- ¾ c. cashews
- 2 tbsp. sesame seeds, ground in coffee grinder
- 1 c. carrots, grated
- 2 c. zucchini, grated
- ¼ c. onion, chopped finely
- 1 cloves, garlic
- 1 c. coconut flour
- 2 tbsp. nutritional yeast (optional)

Directions

Combine ground chia or flax with 2 tablespoons water and set aside for 5 minutes.

In a blender, combine soaked flax/chia seeds, cashews, sesame seeds, onion, garlic, and nutritional yeast until smooth. Add a dash of water, if needed, to make the mixture smoother.

Shred zucchini and carrots and place in a large bowl and combine with the cashew mixture. Add coconut flour and mix until combined into a thick dough.

Spread mixture into dehydrator tray. And dry for about 6 hours flipping and removing the nonstick sheet half way through.

Dry to desired texture, should be dry but not hard.

Fun Fact:

Ancient Greeks and Romans ate carrots but not the orange varieties we know today, they ate wild varieties of various other colors. In the 17th century Dutch carrot growers invented the orange carrot in honor of the House of Orange, the Dutch Royal Family.

Pizza Crust

Preparation: 20 Min. *Drying:* 30-60 Min. *Makes 4-6 Servings*

Ingredients

- 1 c. golden flax seed, ground in a coffee grinder
- 1 c. buckwheat, soaked
- 1 tbs. Himalayan crystal salt
- 1-2 c. pure water
- ¼ c. raw coconut flour (optional)

Directions

Soak buckwheat for at least 1 hour, can soak overnight if desired, drain water and rinse buckwheat. Place buckwheat in a food processor.

Grind flax in a coffee grinder and add to the food processor along with salt and only enough water to make dough.

Roll dough out into a circle, using the coconut flour to keep from sticking. This step could be done with ground flax seed as well.

Place on dehydrator tray and dry for 30-60 minutes at 100°F.

Note

The crust works best if the kitchen is warm.

Fun Facts:

Buckwheat is not cereal grain, grass or related to wheat. Buckwheat is the dried fruit of the plant and is related to rhubarb and sorrel. Buckwheat stabilizes blood sugar levels. After eating buckwheat, sugar level rises slowly, not abruptly. Buckwheat has been shown to protect against cancer. Its flavonoids composition prevents tumor growth. The use of buckwheat helps cleanse blood vessels from the 'bad' cholesterol and prevents the development of cardiovascular disease.

Corn Pizza Crust

Preparation: *Drying:*   *Makes 4-6*
20 Min.   30-60 Min.   *Servings*

Ingredients

- 1 ½ c. buckwheat
- ½ c. gold flax seeds, ground in coffee grinder
- ¼ c. gold flax seeds, whole
- 1 clove garlic
- 1 tsp. basil
- 1 tsp. oregano
- 1 tsp. Himalayan crystal salt
- 1 c. corn
- ½ c. raw coconut flour

Directions

Soak 1 cup of buckwheat overnight. Drain the water off buckwheat.

In a food processor, combine soaked buckwheat, ground flax, whole flax, 2 tablespoons coconut flour, corn, garlic, basil, oregano, and salt. Mix until a thick dough is formed.

Using a coffee grinder, grind ½ cup of dry buckwheat for buckwheat flour.

Use buckwheat flour to thicken dough if it is too sticky in the food processor.

Sprinkle coconut flour on the counter. Knead the dough using more coconut flour if needed until dough is soft and pliable.

Form into pizza crust and place on dehydrator try and dry 30-60 minutes at 100°F.

Note

The crust works best if the kitchen is warm.

Fun Fact:

The ear or cob is part of the flower, while the individual kernel is a seed.

Sweet Pizza Crust

Preparation:	Drying:	Makes 4-6
20 Min.	30-60 Min.	Servings

Ingredients

- ¾ c. pecan, dry
- ¾ c. walnuts, dry
- ½ to 1 c. dates
- 1 tbsp. vanilla
- ¼ to ½ c. date water

Directions

Soak dates in enough pure water to cover for about 20 minutes.

In a food processor, combine walnuts and pecans to a powder or flour. Add pitted dates to nuts and mix until dough is formed.

Form into pizza crust and place on dehydrator try and dry about 1 hour at 100°F.

Note

This recipe works best with dried nuts.

Fun Facts:

1) Vanilla is the only edible fruit of the orchid family. There are over 150 varieties of vanilla plants. Like grapes that make wine, no two vanilla beans are the same in flavor, aroma, or color due to differing soil and climate conditions.

2) In most parts of the world vanilla has to be hand-pollinate since they do not have the Melipona Bee.

3) A few drops of vanilla will cut the acidity of tomato-based foods

4) To accentuate flavors, add a few drops of vanilla to most recipes that contain fruit or vegetables.

Hummus

Preparation:
15 Min.

Ingredients

- 2 c. cashews
- 2 garlic cloves
- 1 tbsp. raw tahini
- 1 lemon, juiced
- 1 tsp. Himalayan crystal salt
- 2 tbsp. cold pressed olive oil (optional)

Directions

Soak cashews for about 15 minutes. Soaking soften the nuts and makes them easier to cream. However, this recipe will work if you skip this step. Drain water off cashews and place them in food processor.

To the food processor with cashews, add, garlic, tahini, salt, lemon, and olive oil blend until well mixed and a paste is formed.

Variation

May use almonds, or sprouted chickpeas in place of cashews.

Almond Lemon Spread

Preparation:
10 Min.

Ingredients

- 1 c. almonds, peeled and soaked overnight
- ½ c. lemon, juiced
- 2 tbsp. lemon zest
- 1 tbsp. coconut nectar
- ½ c. water

Directions

Soak almonds, while wet peel off the brown skin otherwise you will have brown flakes in the lemon spread. Drain water off.

Place peeled almonds in a blender along with lemon zest, lemon juice, stevia leaves, and water. Combine until creamy.

Pizza Crackers

Preparation: 30 Min. Soaking: 2-12 Hrs. Drying: 6-10 Hrs. Makes 6-8 Servings

Ingredients

- 1 c. almonds, soaked overnight
- ½ c. pumpkin seeds, soaked overnight
- 1 red bell pepper
- 1-2 carrots, shredded
- 2-3 stalks celery, sliced
- ¼ c. onion, chopped
- 1 tsp. parsley
- ½ c. raw tahini
- 2 cloves, garlic
- 1 tsp. basil
- 3 tbs. pizza seasoning
- 1 tsp. onion powder
- 1 tbs. Himalayan crystal salt
- 1 tsp. cold pressed olive oil
- pure water as needed

Directions

Soak almonds and pumpkin seeds overnight. Drain water off and place almonds and pumpkin seeds in a food processor.

Cut and seed bell pepper. Slice celery into small pieces. Place the bell pepper, celery, carrots, parsley, garlic, olive oil, tahini, and spices in the food processor and combine until mixed. Add only enough water as needed to make sure everything combines.

Spread to about a half an inch thick on a nonstick dehydrator sheet. lightly cut into desired shape. Dehydrate at 100°F for about 3 hours.

Flip and carefully remove the nonstick dehydrator sheet. Continue drying in the dehydrator until desired moisture is obtained approximately 4 more hours.

Nadhirrah's Baykon

Preparation: 15 Min. Marinating: 2-24 Hrs. Drying: 12-18 Hrs. Makes 4-6 Servings

Ingredients

- 2 large Asian eggplants
- ¼-½ c. cold pressed olive oil
- 2 tbsp. raw apple cider vinegar
- 1 grapefruit, juiced
- 3 tbsp. Himalayan crystal salt

Directions

Cut off the top and bottom of the eggplant. While you can use any kind of eggplant, the long thin Asian eggplant will look more like bacon.

Using a mandolin, thinly slice eggplant lengthwise. It should be long strips of thin eggplant.

Place a layer of sliced eggplant on bottom of marinating pan. Sprinkle some salt over the top of that layer. Add another layer of sliced eggplant, add more salt continue until the eggplant is all laid out.

Pour olive oil over the top of the eggplant, add vinegar and grapefruit juice. If the eggplant is not covered, then add more oil and vinegar. If it's still not covered, use a little bit of water.

Marinate for at least 2 hours and up to 24 hours. The eggplant may darken. That is okay; it is just oxidation.

Using dehydrator trays, place marinated baykon out to dry in single layers.

Dehydrate about 18 hours. Baykon should be crispy when done.

Note

For easy clean up, place a nonstick dehydrator sheet on the bottom of the dehydrator to catch dripping oil.

Irish Moss Gel

Ingredients

- 1 c. Irish moss
- 2-3 c. pure water

Directions

Rinse Irish moss. Soak in water for 30 minutes. Drain and rinse again then soak in fresh water overnight in a glass jar, then drain water.

Place Irish moss in a blender with just enough fresh water to cover. Blend until smooth, it may take a few minutes.

Pour into a clean jar with a lid. Store in refrigerator up to 3 weeks.

> **Fun Fact:**
>
> Irish Moss is a tough and stringy seaweed growing that grows on rocks in tidal pools along the northern Atlantic.
>
> Irish Moss is so nutrient dense that it was used as "poverty food" during the famous Irish Potato Famine of 1846 – 1848. It is thought that this contributed to its fall from favor after the famine.

Guacamole

Preparation: 15 Min.
Makes 4-6 Servings

Ingredients

- ¼ c. mayo (page 80)
- 1-2 large avocados
- Himalayan crystal salt

Directions

Make mayo and set aside.

Cut avocados and remove meat from the shell and place on a plate. Add mayo and salt to the avocado and mix with a fork.

Rejuvelac

| Preparation: | Sprouting: | Fermenting: | Makes 1 |
| 10 Min. | 1-3 Days | 2-4 Days | Gallon |

Ingredients

- 1 c. sprouted wheat, ½ -1 inch tail
- 1 gallon water

Directions

Sprout wheat for one to 3 days. The wheat should have a ½ -1 inch tail.

Drain soaking water and place wheat in a food processor. Add 2 cups of pure water and pulse the blender for 2-3 minutes until everything is well blended.

Pour into a gallon picture and add the remaining water. Stir the liquid and then cover with the cheesecloth.

Stir the liquid 2 to 4 times a day for 2 to 3 days. You should have a slightly lemony flavor when done. If it stinks really bad, it is no good.

Refrigerate after the fermentation time.

> **Fun Fact:**
>
> Rejuvelac is a general term for a fermented liquid used to improve digestion of food.

Almond Sour Cream

Preparation: 15 Min.   *Makes 4-6 Servings*

Ingredients

- 1 c. almonds, soaked overnight and peeled
- 1 tsp. lemon juice
- 1 tbsp. raw apple cider vinegar
- ½ c. pure water as needed
- Himalayan crystal salt to taste

Directions

Soak almonds overnight. While the brown skins are still wet, peel them off. This is done in order to have a white sour cream. If the skin is left on the almonds you will have a brown flaked sour cream.

In a blender, combine peeled almonds, lemon juice, raw apple cider vinegar, and salt. Purée until it is creamy adding only enough water as needed to thin.

Taste and adjust seasoning you may need more lemon or vinegar if it's not sour enough.

Almond Mayo

Preparation: 10 Min. *Soaking:* 8-12 Hrs. *Makes 6-8 Servings*

Ingredients

- 2 c. almonds, soaked overnight and peeled
- 3 tbsp. onion powder
- ½ c. cold pressed olive oil
- ¾ c. water
- 1-2 tbsp. Himalayan crystal salt
- ½ lemon, juiced

Directions

Cover almonds with water, soak overnight and drain. While still wet peel the brown shell off each almond.

Place peeled almonds into a blender and add olive oil, onion powder, salt, and lemon juice.

Slowly blend adding enough water until a creamy, mayo consistency is achieved.

Variations

For **cashew mayo** substitute cashew nuts for almonds. Cashews can become rubbery, so I usually do not soak them very long if at all.

This recipe can be used with almost any nut or seed you can think of. For example, hazelnut, pumpkin seeds, walnuts etc.

Fun Fact:

"Expeller Pressed" is a continuous feed method where oil is squeezed from the raw material in one step under high pressure. All cold pressed oil is expeller pressed, but not all expeller pressed oil is cold pressed. If the bottle says expeller pressed, it may or may not have been processed under high heat. The only way to know for sure is to call the manufacturer or the label clearly states "cold pressed".

Almond Milk

Preparation: *Soaking:*   *Makes 6-8*
5 Min.   *8-12 Hrs.*   *Servings*

Ingredients

- 1 c. almonds, soaked overnight and peel
- 2 c. pure water

Directions

Soak almonds overnight. Drain off the water while wet peel off brown skin. Place almonds into a blender with 2 cups of pure freshwater. Blend for a minute or two.

Using a milk bag, clean nylon sock, or cheesecloth, over a big bowl pour the contents of the blender into the bag.

Squeeze the liquid out of the milk bag. That liquid is now your milk. Sweeten milk if desired.

Note

Use the almond pulp in another recipe such as almond mayo, cookies, crackers or bread to peel the brown skin off.

Variation

Nut milk can be made with any nut or seed that you can imagine examples with the Brazil nuts, pumpkin seeds, sesame seed, and hazelnut just name a few.

Cashew Cream

Preparation:
10 Min.

Ingredients

- 2 c. cashews
- 1 ½ c. pure water
- ½ c. raw liquid sweetener
- ¼ inch vanilla bean or raw vanilla powder

Directions

In a blender, combine cashew nuts, orange juice, raw liquid sweetener, and vanilla. Add just enough water to achieve a very creamy texture.

Spicy Cheese

Preparation: 15 Min.   Soaking: 8-12 Hrs.   Makes 6-8 Servings

Ingredients

- 1 c. almonds, soaked overnight
- ¼ c. lemon juice
- ½ tsp. Himalayan crystal salt or sea salt
- 1 tsp. dill
- 1 green onion, chopped
- 1 red bell pepper, diced
- 1 chili pepper
- ½ c. tomatoes

Directions

Soak almonds overnight. Drain water off the almonds.

In a small bowl place or dried tomatoes and olive oil and water let soak for 30 min. You can use fresh tomatoes if they are available. You will want to save the water from the tomatoes to use if needed but don't use the almond water.

In a food processor placed the almonds, lemon juice, salt, dill, green onion, red bell pepper, and chili pepper. Process until well mixed. Add the dried tomatoes and blend until the tomatoes have been incorporated. Chill and serve.

Serving suggestion serve on a flax cracker or other raw cracker or as a dip with vegetables.

Note

For a smoother cheese use a blender in place of food processor.

Fun Fact:

Vegan cheeses are made from a variety of plant-based ingredients.

Rawmesan

Preparation: 15 Min.
Makes 4-6 Servings

Ingredients

- ½ c. cashews
- ¼ c. raw, pumpkin seeds
- ½ tsp. Himalayan crystal salt
- ½ tsp. dill
- ½ tbsp. nutritional yeast (optional)

Directions

In a food processor, grind cashews and pumpkin seed into a powder. Add salt and dill and pulse a few more times.

Rawmesan will keep about a month in the refrigerator.

Fun Fact:

Parmesan is an Italian cheese this nut and seed mixture replaces the feel of parmesan cheese.

Gorgonzola Style Cheese

Preparation: 15 Min. *Soaking:* 8-12 Hrs. *Makes 6-8 Servings*

Ingredients

- ¼ c. Irish moss gel (page 77)
- ¼-¾ c. water
- 1 c. raw cashews
- ¼ tsp. Himalayan crystal salt
- ¼ c. unrefined coconut oil
- 4 tbsp. lemon juice
- 1 tbsp. raw apple cider vinegar
- 2 tbsp. tahini
- 1 tbsp. onion, chopped
- 1 garlic clove
- ¼ tsp. spirulina

Directions

Make Irish moss gel.

Place Irish moss gel, cashews, lemon, and salt blend until smooth. Adding water as needed to achieve smoothness.

Drain and press the mixture to release liquid. Return to blender.

Peace coconut oil, lemon juice, raw apple cider vinegar, tahini, onion powder, and garlic powder in a blender until smooth.

Transfer the mixture to bowl, dot cheese with spirulina using a toothpick. Fold cheese over a few times to create the blue-green veins.

Place the cheese mixture in a cheese cloth with ends wrapped up. Hang cheese ball over a container cover and refrigerate for 6-8 hours to firm and set.

Fun Fact:

Spirulina is blue-green algae. Spirulina is one of the few plant sources of vitamin B12 and is 65 to 71 percent complete protein, with all essential amino acids in perfect balance. In comparison, beef is only 22 percent protein.

Ricotta Cheese Sauce

Preparation: 15 Min. *Makes 4-6 Servings*

Ingredients

- 1 c. macadamia nuts
- 2 cloves garlic
- 1 ½ tsp. Himalayan crystal salt
- 2 tsp. Italian seasoning
- ½ c. zucchini
- ½ c. water or more as needed

Directions

In a blender, puree the macadamia nuts, garlic, zucchini, and spice until fluffy using as little water as possible. Should look like a cheese sauce.

Fun Fact:

Almond Milk is all the rage. But in the middle ages it was even more popular with the upper class.

The first mention almond milk appears in a medical context in the 12th century and quickly spread from the Mediterranean to Germany, England and Denmark.

Cookbook from the middle ages use almond milk as staple food and not just an alternative ingredient.

In the middle ages during lent when European Christians abstained from dairy, they drank almond milk.

Medieval chefs were fond of coloring their dishes, so almond milk's blank-white canvas became an ideal outlet for this self-expression.

Almond milk was easier to digest, and the medieval doctors thought it was easier on an invalid's system. For the less well-off, falling ill could give one the chance to indulge in the aristocratic delights of almond milk.

Vegan Fruit Cream Cheese

Preparation: 20 Min. Makes 2-4 Servings

Ingredients

- ½ c. cashews, soaked for 10 minutes
- ½ c. macadamia nuts, soaked for 10 minutes
- 1 lemons, juiced
- ½ tsp. Himalayan crystal salt
- ½ c. fresh fruit (strawberries, raspberry, pineapple, blueberry or other fruit choice)
- 1 tbsp. coconut oil
- ¼ c. rejuvelac or water

Directions

Soak cashews and macadamia nuts for 10 minutes. Drain off the water and place nuts into a food processor add lemon juice and mix until smooth.

Wash chosen fruit and place in the food processor mix the fruit in until the desired texture is achieved, this can be big chunks or very smooth.

Place in a dish and cover. Chill for about an hour or until ready to serve. Can store in a sealed container for 4-7 days.

Variations

For plain cream cheese omit fruit.

Note

Can be made with all cashews if desired.

Fun Fact:

Up to two-thirds of the global population are lactose intolerant. Unlike food allergies, lactose intolerance isn't immunity-related. It comes from the body's inability to digest lactose, the primary sugar in cow's milk.

Herbed Vegan Cream Cheese

Preparation: 20 Min. *Soaking:* 2-8 hrs. *Makes* 2-4 Servings

Ingredients

- ½ c. cashews
- ½ c. pumpkin seeds, soaked overnight
- 2 lemons, juiced
- ½ tsp. Himalayan crystal salt
- ¼ tsp. nutritional yeast (optional)
- ½ tsp. chives
- ½ tsp. dried oregano
- ½ tsp. dried parsley
- ½ tsp. dried basil
- ¼ tsp. dried dill

Directions

Soak pumpkin seeds overnight. Drain off the water. Pace seeds in a food processor.

Soak cashews for 10 minutes. Drain off the water and add to pumpkin seeds.

Juice lemons and add the juice to a food processor along with salt, nutritional yeast, chives, oregano, parsley, basil and dill then process until smooth. Add water a tablespoon at a time to thin the mixture if needed.

Place in a dish and cover. Chill for about an hour or until ready to serve. Can store in a sealed container for 4-7 days.

Note

Can be made with all cashews if desired.

Fun Fact:

Dairy-free cheese has a history dating back to 16th century China.

Basic Seed Cheese

Preparation: 30 Min. Makes 4-6 Servings

Ingredients

- 1 c. sunflower seeds
- 1 c. pumpkin seeds
- 1 c. rejuvelac

Directions

Soak pumpkin and sunflower seeds overnight, drain off water and set seeds aside.

Pour rejuvelac and half the seeds into a blender, blend at high speed until well blended. Add remaining seeds to the blender and combine until it is a smooth thick paste about 4 minutes.

Pour mixture into cheese cloth wrap edges of cloth together and hand over a bowl or jar cover with a clean towel or cloth, and leave it for 8-12 hours. The longer it stands, the stronger the flavor.

After fermentation time elapses, discard liquid that has settled at the bottom of the jar. Store extra cheese in refrigerator tightly cover.

Variations

1) May replace the rejuvelac with the juice of 1 lemon, 1 tablespoon raw apple cider vinegar and 1 cup pure water

2) Try making this cheese with almonds. Combinations of almonds, sunflower seeds, and sesame are also very flavorful.

Fun Fact:

Homemade vegan cheeses can be made with nuts and seeds. Some of the most popular ingredients for nut and seed based cheeses include, macadamia nuts, almonds, pecans, pine nuts, sunflower seeds, pumpkin seeds.

Vegan Feta Cheese

Preparation: 30 Min. *Makes 4-6 Servings*

Ingredients

- 1 c. almonds, soaked overnight
- ¼ c. fresh basil or thyme, oregano or other spice, chopped
- ¼ tsp. Himalayan crystal salt
- ¾ c. rejuvelac

Directions

Soak almonds overnight drain water off. Peel brown skin off the almonds while wet. Place peeled almonds in a blender.

Pour rejuvelac into the blender with almonds and salt. Blend at high speed, until smooth.

Chop fresh basil and pulse in blender or mix by hand. If using the blender make sure that it only pulsed otherwise you will have a green cheese.

Pour blender mixture into cheese cloth over a bowl or glass jar. Wrap the edges of the cloth and gently squeeze liquid out. Hang wrapped cheese over the bowl, and leave it for 8-12 hours. The longer it stands the stronger the flavor will be.

After the fermentation, time elapses, discard any liquid that has settle in the bowl or jar. Store extra cheese in the refrigerator tightly covered.

Variation

If you don't have Rejuvelac, you can use lemon, and a half a cup of water instead. If you use this method the fermentation time may need to be extended to 12 -18 hours.

Fun Fact:

Herbs have been used from the beginning of time to flavor food and as medicine. The leaves, seeds, bark, root, and flowers are used.

Index

A

Almond Lemon Spread 73
Almond Mayo 80
Almond Milk 81
Almond Pizza Crust 10
Almond Sour Cream 79
Apple Pie Pizza 52
Artichoke Zucchini Pizza 17
Avocado Pizza 49

B

Basic Seed Cheese 88
Baykon 76
BBQ Pizza 34
BBQ Sauce 35
Blackberry Basil Pizza 21
Brazil nut Crust 46
Brownie Pizza 56
Brussels Sprouts Pizza 24

C

Carrot Tops Herb Pizza 50
Cashew Cream 81
Cashew Mayo 80
Cauliflower Pizza Crust 66
Chocolate Pudding Pizza 65
Cinnamon Roll Pizza 62
Coconut Berry Pizza 55
Corn Pizza Crust 71
Cream Cheese 86

D

Dragon Pizza 60

E

Easy Vegetable Pizza 45

F

Feta Cheese 89
Fresh Pizza 10
Fruit Cream Cheese 86
Fruit Pizza 58

G

Garlic Sauce 35
Ginger Pizza Crust 60
Gorgonzola Style Cheese 84
Greek dressing 23
Greek Pizza 23
Green Pizza 32
Guacamole 77

H

Herved Vegan
      Cream Cheese 87
Hummus 73
Hummus Pizza 33

I

Irish Moss Gel 77

J

Jalapeno Popper Pizza 41
Jamaican Jerk
      Zucchini Pizza 14

K

Kale Pizza 9
Kale Pizza Crust 68
Kohlrabi Pizza Crust 67

L

Lemon Pizza 28
Lemon Spread 73

M

Mayo 80
Meet-za Pizza 46
Mint Chocolate
    Pudding Pizza 65

N

Nadhirrah's Baykon 76
Nut Mayo 80
Nut milk 81

O

Olive Pizza 5
Olive Pizza on
    Zucchini Carrot Crust 44

P

Pear and Gorgonzola Style
    Cheese Pizza 20
Pesto Pizza 18
Philly Pizza 12
Pizza Appetizer 33
Pizza Bites 6

Pizza Crackers 74
Pizza Crust 70
Plain Cream Cheese 86

R

Rawmesan 83
Rejuvelac 78
Ricotta Cheese Sauce 85

S

Seed Cheese 88
Sour Cream 79
Spicy Brazil Nut
    Zausage Pizza 36
Spicy Cheese 82
Spinach - Kohlrabi Pizza 42
Sweet Pizza Crust 72

T

Taco Pizza 27
Tomato and Basil Pizza 30

V

Vegan Feta Cheese 89
Vegan Fruit Cream Cheese 86
Veggie Ranch Pizza 29

Z

Zausage Pizza 36
Zuccheroni Pizza 38
Zucchini Carrot Pizza Crust 69
Zucchini Pepperoni Pizza 38

About the Author

Kachina Choate, a long-time vegetarian, ironically didn't like vegetables. She stood up one day and said, "I'm tired of eating food that tastes like twigs, weeds, and Styrofoam--there has to be a better way."

Since then, she has been creating and serving healthy food to her unsuspecting friends who--when they find out the food is raw & fresh, have said, "I can't believe I ate something healthy... and liked it!"

She is the author of In the Season Thereof, 101 ½ Raw Zucchinis and What to do With Them, Pumpkins Do Grow on Trees, Thriving on Plant-Based Food Storage, The Beautiful Soup and Salad Book, The Pizza Book and Kachina Summer Bear Recipe Card Collection.

She began her natural, unprocessed, raw food journey in 2002, and as a result, has recovered from depression and kicked a pernicious sugar addiction. She loves to travel and teach healthy food that tastes delicious.

She started Summer Bear Life Balance Education, a non-profit organization to help people achieve health and balanced life.

Website: SummerBear.org
Facebook: SummerBearLifeBalance
Instagram: summer_bear_org
Pinterest:
dollkachina/raw-food-wfpb-food-storage-by-summerbearorg
dollkachina/kachina-summer-bears-raw-foods